Who Is
Ruth Bader Ginsburg?

Who Is
Ruth Bader Ginsburg?

by Patricia Brennan Demuth

illustrated by Jake Murray

Penguin Workshop

For Ileah Brennan, a reading wonder,
and her talented mom, Megan, Esq.
You make our world shine—PBD

For my sister, Sara—JM

PENGUIN WORKSHOP
An Imprint of Penguin Random House LLC, New York

Visit us online at www.penguinrandomhouse.com.

Library of Congress Cataloging-in-Publication Data is available upon request.

ISBN 9781524793531 (paperback)   10 9 8 7 6 5 4 3 2 1
ISBN 9781524793548 (library binding)   10 9 8 7 6 5 4 3 2 1

Contents

Who Is Ruth Bader Ginsburg?

Like every kid, Ruth always looked forward to her birthday. When the special day came along, she and her mother loaded up bags of ice cream. Then they brought the treats to the place where Ruth celebrated all her birthdays. It wasn't filled with balloons or wrapped presents. It was at a nearby orphanage—a home for children who didn't have parents.

Sometimes Ruth wished for birthday parties like her friends had. But the smiles on the children always changed her mind.

Life wasn't always easy for Ruth's family, either. Her parents were hardworking immigrants. They rented an apartment in Brooklyn, New York. But Ruth's mother taught her to care for others who had even less. It made Ruth want to "do something" when she grew up—something to change people's lives.

But how could a girl make a big difference? When Ruth was a child, girls faced lots of closed doors. Back then, there were police*men*, mail*men*, and fire*men*. Doctors, dentists, pilots, lawyers, soldiers—nearly all were male.

Ruth never dreamed that one day she'd beat the odds and become a lawyer. But that's what she did. And it was just the beginning.

Ruth was tiny, soft-spoken, and always polite. Yet when it came to standing up for people's rights, she was a warrior. She fought to change laws to give women an equal chance in society.

One by one, she opened doors. Then she walked right through many of those open doors herself—all the way to the Supreme Court!

Today, Ruth Bader Ginsburg is so famous that millions know her just from her initials: RBG.

What Is the Supreme Court?

The Supreme Court sits in Washington, DC, our nation's capital. It's part of the judicial branch of government. The other two branches are the legislative branch (Congress) and the executive branch (which includes the president). A group of nine judges, called justices, sit on the Court. There are no juries. The justices have the final say on matters of law in the United States.

From left to right:
Elena Kagan, Samuel A. Alito Jr., Ruth Bader Ginsburg,
Brett M. Kavanaugh, John G. Roberts Jr. (Chief Justice)

The framers of the Constitution wanted the Supreme Court to be independent of politics. So justices are allowed to hold their jobs for life. They can't be removed for making unpopular decisions.

The Supreme Court has a big job to do. It makes sure the Constitution is followed by Congress, the president, and all fifty states. Its decisions affect the lives of all Americans.

Clarence Thomas, Stephen G. Breyer, Sonia Sotomayor, Neil M. Gorsuch

CHAPTER 1
An Immigrant Family

The future judge known as RBG was born a frisky baby on March 15, 1933. Her birth name was Joan Ruth Bader. But as a baby, she kicked so much that her big sister, Marilyn, nicknamed her Kiki (say: KICK-ee). Later, at school, she started going by her middle name because there were so many Joans in her class. Ruth was the name that stuck.

Ruth grew up in Brooklyn, a bustling part of New York City. She lived with her parents, Nathan and Celia Bader, on the bottom floor of a two-family house. Their landlady lived right above them. Their block was filled with hardworking immigrant families like theirs.

Ruth's shy, gentle father had been born in Ukraine (near Russia). Nathan was forbidden from going to school there because he was Jewish. In the United States, he went to night school to learn English and become a citizen.

Ruth's mother, Celia, was born in America just months after her family arrived from Poland. They were also fleeing because they were Jewish. Young Ruth learned early from her parents to treasure America's freedoms.

Like the other fathers in the neighborhood, Nathan Bader left for work each morning. Nathan made a living selling fur hats and coats.

But in the 1930s, during the Great Depression, most Americans were too broke to afford them. Nathan had to work late just to make ends meet.

Celia stayed home to raise her two daughters. Sadly, when Ruth was two, her six-year-old sister died. After that, Celia pinned all her hopes on little Ruth.

Immigrants in New York City

Millions of immigrants flooded into the United States at the beginning of the 1900s. Terrible hardships, including religious prejudice, drove most immigrants to leave their homelands. About one-third of the newcomers stayed right in New York, where they first landed at Ellis Island.

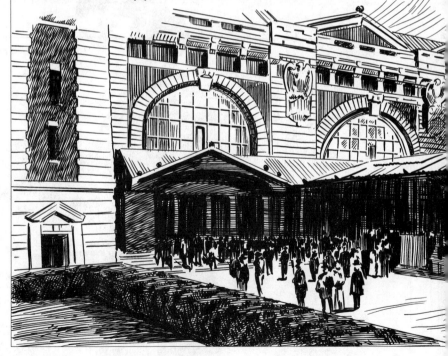

Ellis Island

At that time, most mothers hoped their daughters would grow up to marry some Prince Charming. Not Celia. She believed in women's rights. As a young woman, she had marched in a parade to get women the right to vote. She raised her daughter to be independent. More than anything, she wanted Ruth to get a good education.

Celia had been a brilliant student herself. She graduated from high school at age fifteen! She dreamed of going to college. But Celia's father thought college was wasted on a girl. So Celia took an office job instead. Every week, she handed over money to help her older brother attend college. Now, as a mother, she passed along a love of books and learning to her daughter. Ruth's earliest memory was of sitting on her mother's lap while Celia read to her.

Ruth became a good student like her mother. Sometimes, though, she felt a lot of pressure.

One time, her report card showed a poor grade. Her mother looked so disappointed. Ruth made up her mind to get straight As from then on. And she did.

Life wasn't all about studying, though. Not by any means. Outdoors, the kids on the block played in a pack. Jumping rope was the rage with girls then. Ruth could jump double dutch, quickly stepping in and out of two long ropes swinging in opposite directions. Some days, she explored the neighborhood on her roller skates.

One day Ruth watched five boys from the block leaping from one garage roof to another. That looked fun and daring! Jumping roofs wasn't at all "ladylike." But that didn't stop lively Ruth from joining in.

As a child, Ruth also found a passion for the arts. Her "dream place" was the Brooklyn Academy of Music, just a subway ride away. Every Saturday,

Brooklyn Academy of Music, 1930s

her mother took her to see children's theater there. With her class, Ruth went on school trips to see the art collection at the Brooklyn Museum.

When Ruth turned eleven, her mother took her to her first opera. Opera is like a play, only all the parts are sung. Ruth thought it was magnificent! The soaring voices, the music, the costumes, the drama—it all thrilled her. She dreamed of being an opera star. But her voice was so bad that her teacher asked Ruth not to sing out loud in chorus!

Once a week, Celia dropped Ruth off at the library while she got her hair done. Ruth curled up in a chair and read stories of daring women.

Her favorites were the Nancy Drew mysteries starring a smart, independent girl detective. The real-life story of Amelia Earhart, a famous pilot,

Amelia Earhart

fired her imagination, too. Right below the library was a Chinese restaurant. Delicious smells drifted up while Ruth lost herself in reading. From then on, the smells of soy sauce and egg rolls reminded Ruth of books.

In 1945, when Ruth was twelve, World War II ended with Germany's defeat. Adolf Hitler's plan had been to rule all of Europe and wipe out the Jews. As a Jewish girl, Ruth was very aware that

Jews were being killed by Hitler's forces. Her own family was safe in America. Yet even in the United States, there was prejudice.

On a trip to Pennsylvania, Ruth spotted a sign outside a hotel: NO DOGS OR JEWS ALLOWED, it read. Many years later, when she was a judge, Ruth would tell the US Senate about the sting of those words.

A Woman's Right to Vote

For decades, women in the United States worked hard to win the right to vote. But it wasn't until 1920 that an amendment—or change—to the United States Constitution made it a law that women would be allowed to vote. Since women make up more than half of the US population today, their votes can determine the outcome of many elections.

CHAPTER 2
A Terrible Secret

By the time Ruth got to high school, it was clear she'd always be small. She never grew past five feet tall or weighed more than a hundred pounds. Yet Ruth aimed big. That was clear when she chose to play one of the largest instruments in the high-school orchestra—the cello.

James Madison High School was an enormous redbrick schoolhouse, five stories high. Even among her eight hundred classmates, Ruth stood out. She was soon earning straight As. You would think she would have been super confident. But she worried over every test.

As for team sports, Ruth couldn't play any because there weren't any teams for girls! Even cheerleaders at Madison High were boys. So, after learning to twirl a baton, Ruth joined the Go-Getters pep club. On football game nights, she and the other Go-Getters cheered and twirled for their school team.

Title IX

Before 1972, public schools were not required to have sports for girls. Then Title IX was passed. (In Roman numerals, *IX* stands for "nine.") From then on, any education program that got money from the government had to provide equal sports opportunities for girls. Before Title IX, only one out of every twenty-seven girls competed in sports. Today, two girls out of every five take part.

Ruth also found time to edit the school newspaper and date boys. Outwardly, she appeared to not have a care in the world. But she was holding in a big secret.

Her mother had cancer. Ruth never told a soul, not even her closest friends. She didn't want anyone feeling sorry for her.

Celia had many operations and was in the hospital for weeks at a time. At home between surgeries, Celia was usually bedridden. Every night, Ruth sat beside her and did homework.

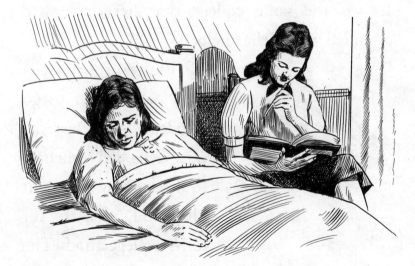

She knew it comforted her mother to see her studying.

In 1950, the spring of her senior year, Ruth was asked to give a speech at her graduation ceremony. Ruth, however, never went to graduation. Her beloved mother died the day before. Losing her mother was a terrible blow. Ruth felt devastated.

She had to push herself forward, the way Celia would have wanted her to do. College, her mother's dream for her, lay just three months ahead. Ruth would be going to Cornell University. It was the same college that her uncle had attended with Celia's help.

To Ruth's surprise, Celia helped pay for her to go to college, too. Over the years, Celia had somehow squirreled away eight thousand dollars for Ruth's college fund. The family discovered the nest egg after Celia's death. It was a huge sum! Celia had been one strong, determined woman.

She had raised her daughter to be the same way.

CHAPTER 3
Opposites Attract

Cornell University was nothing at all like Ruth's city high school. The hilly campus spread over two thousand acres in upstate New York. A lake sparkled below. Wooded paths wound around ivy-covered buildings. Still, Ruth soon fit right in.

It was easy to like Ruth. She was soft-spoken and kind. She was pretty, with long, soft dark hair and big blue eyes. And she was "crazy smart." Her friends were in awe of Ruth's laser focus. "You could drop a bomb over her head and she wouldn't know it," one classmate said. When the dorm got too noisy, Ruth escaped to a bathroom stall to study!

For a while, Ruth had no clear career goal. Then she became aware of something troubling that was taking place in the US Senate.

A "Red Scare"—an extreme fear of all communists—was sweeping across the United States. A senator named Joe McCarthy was taking advantage of people's fears. McCarthy accused many decent Americans of being traitors to the United States—of wanting to destroy the country. He hauled them into the Senate for hearings. And he threatened them with prison if they didn't turn over their friends. Careers were ended, and lives were ruined.

Senator Joe McCarthy

Who could stand up for the accused? Lawyers could and did. They defended citizens' right to free speech. (The Constitution says you can believe whatever you want.)

What Does a Lawyer Do?

Any American who is accused of breaking a law is entitled to a fair trial. Some people will defend themselves in court. But most have a lawyer represent them because lawyers have been trained to understand the legal system.

Not all lawyers are trial lawyers. And not all

lawyers take on criminal cases. Some help people draw up contracts when they buy a house, make a will, or get a divorce. Ruth's future husband became a tax lawyer who helped clients—often big companies—work through complicated tax problems. Ruth became a constitutional lawyer who took on cases about citizens' rights in the United States.

For the first time, Ruth began to think a career in law might be right for her.

Lots of guys at Cornell had asked Ruth on dates. They were nice, but no one interested her very much. Not until Marty Ginsburg came along.

Marty was Ruth's opposite. He was outgoing, the life of every party. Ruth was quiet and shy. He was tall; she was short. Ruth was serious. Fun-loving Marty cracked jokes and made Ruth laugh. Together, they just clicked. Marty and Ruth proved the old saying "opposites attract."

In the 1950s, girls at Cornell often felt they had to hide how smart they were. At that time, boys didn't seem to like brainy girls because most guys looked for wives to take care of housework and children while they made a living. Not Marty Ginsburg. He loved Ruth's lively mind and her desire for a career of her own. "Marty was the first boy I ever knew who cared that I had a brain," said Ruth.

Soon the two were talking about a future together—a future in which they would both be lawyers. But a lady lawyer?! There were few in the 1950s. So what? Ruth made up her mind to go for it, anyway. Aiming high, Marty and Ruth both applied to Harvard University. Harvard accepted them both!

Since he was a year older, Marty started at Harvard while Ruth stayed to finish at Cornell. She graduated in 1954—number one among the female students!

Just a few days later, she married her sweetheart. From then on, her name was Ruth Bader Ginsburg. Years later, Ruth would say, "Meeting Marty was by far the most fortunate thing that ever happened to me."

As things turned out, law school had to wait awhile for the Ginsburgs. The couple headed instead to an army base in Oklahoma. Marty had been called on to serve two years at Fort Sill.

Sharpshooting Marty liked teaching at the army artillery school. But Ruth had some trouble at her desk job at the Social Security office.

One day she told her boss she was pregnant. The news had overjoyed Ruth and Marty—but not her boss. He cut her salary and lowered her job rank. Bosses back then didn't think pregnant

women belonged in the workplace. Schools and businesses often fired pregnant women on the spot. There were no laws to protect these women. For now, Ruth stayed quiet. That would certainly change later!

A few months later, Ruth and Marty welcomed a baby daughter. They named her Jane. The new

parents became pioneers in a new kind of family life. They shared family chores as equal partners. Even though Marty worked full-time, he didn't expect Ruth to do all the parenting. After all, she worked, too. Marty shopped, cleaned, and helped care for the baby. Plus, he took over the cooking. Ruth couldn't cook a tasty dish no matter what!

After two years in Oklahoma, it was time to leave and go to law school. But worries ate at Ruth. Jane was just a year old. Other mothers at that time stayed home to raise their children. Maybe she should, too, and give up her dream of becoming a lawyer.

Her father-in-law helped Ruth decide. He told her it was perfectly fine if she wanted to stay home. But, if her heart was set on law school, she should

stop worrying and find a way to make it happen.

"That was wonderful advice that I followed all my life," Ruth later recalled. When a decision came up, she would ask herself, "Do I want this enough? If I do, then I could find a way."

CHAPTER 4
Law School

Ruth didn't shine at everything she tried. She couldn't sing or cook. And she flunked her driver's test five times before passing it. But at law, Ruth proved to be a natural. Soon she stood out in her class as a star student.

That wasn't the only reason she stood out at Harvard Law School in 1956. It was also because she was female. There were only nine women in her class—and more than five hundred men!

None of the teachers were female. Harvard Law had only started accepting women students a few years earlier. The large classroom building still had no women's bathroom. Ruth sometimes had to make a mad dash for a makeshift restroom a block away.

Being the only girl in a class was hard, especially for shy Ruth. She felt like she was always on display. Even worse, she was afraid of giving a wrong answer. That might make men think women were unfit to become lawyers.

Almost all of Ruth's classmates—men and

women—were single. They had nothing else to do but study, day and night. Ruth had a toddler at home to care for. Even with Marty's help, she couldn't afford to waste a minute of time.

This was her routine:

8:30 a.m.—Leave for school when the nanny came. Attend classes and study all day.

4:00 p.m.—Return home for baby time. Change diapers, read storybooks to Jane, and play silly games.

7:00 p.m.—Put Jane to bed. Then hit the books.

Did motherhood hold Ruth back at Harvard? Not one bit. Time with her child cleared her mind and gave her energy to study hard later. Ruth rose straight to the top of her law class. Then, as if out of the blue, a crisis struck. Marty learned he had cancer. The disease was already very advanced. Massive radiation treatments had to begin immediately.

It was crushing news. But Ruth refused to lose hope or let herself feel overwhelmed. Together, she and Marty got through one treatment at a time, then the next.

The treatments made Marty so ill, he couldn't attend classes. So Ruth asked Marty's friends to share their class notes with him. Then, after tucking Jane into bed, Ruth typed up the notes for Marty. She also typed his papers and took over his share of household chores. It was long past midnight before she found time to tackle her own law-school work.

A juggling act like this was nearly impossible to keep up. Something had to give. For Ruth, it was sleep. She grabbed only a couple of hours of sleep before the alarm clock rang in the morning. This routine became a habit for her. For the rest of her life, Ruth worked very, very late and slept very, very little.

Against all odds, Marty beat cancer and he graduated from Harvard right on time. A large law firm in New York City offered Marty a job. That meant Ruth faced a tough choice. She either had to leave Harvard Law School in Boston or stay there without Marty. In the end, it was most important to Ruth to keep her family together. So she spent her last year of law school at Columbia University in New York City.

In the spring of 1959, Ruth graduated. All her hard work had paid off. She tied for number one in her class!

At graduation, a three-year-old in the audience watched as Ruth received her diploma. Suddenly, the child stood up and yelled, "That's my mommy!"

Of course, it was proud little Jane Ginsburg.

CHAPTER 5
Changing Times

Each spring, big law firms compete to hire graduates from the best law schools in the country. Ruth was an outstanding student. She had graduated at the very top of her class at a top law school. Job offers were bound to flood in. Right?

Wrong! Not a single one came! On their job postings, law firms stated "MEN ONLY." Ten, twenty, thirty . . . more than forty firms rejected her application!

Not only was she female, but Ruth also had another strike against her: She was a mother. Bosses didn't think a young mom could put in long hours like men did. Finally, with the help of one of her law professors, Ruth landed a job working as a clerk (assistant) to a federal judge.

Then, in 1963, a new path opened for Ruth. Rutgers University in New Jersey hired her to teach law. She became one of the few female law professors in the nation.

There was one catch: Her pay was less than that of the male teachers. Men needed more money in order to support their families, the dean explained. Ruth asked if that meant a single man with no children would also get paid less. The answer was no. To Ruth, that didn't make sense. And it was totally unfair. But Ruth stayed quiet . . . for now.

And she stayed quiet a while later when she found out she was pregnant again. Privately, she and Marty were thrilled! But at work, she hid the good news behind loose clothes. She wasn't about to risk another pay cut or losing her job.

Ruth and Marty's son, James, was born in 1965.

Big sister Jane was already ten. The Ginsburg household was busier than ever.

Teaching law suited Ruth. As years passed, she began seeing more and more women filling her law classes. America was changing. During the 1960s and 1970s, the women's movement swept the nation. Women joined the workforce

in record numbers. Many didn't want to stay at home with children full-time. They now wanted motherhood *and* a career. Women started to demand entry into "men only" jobs and schools. At rallies and marches, they called for the right to be treated as equal citizens.

Ruth's generation had accepted the way things were. But now Ruth got ready to fight, too—only not in marches or at sit-ins. She was ready to fight in the courtroom! Many laws across the country treated women unfairly. Ruth understood that even if society was changing, old-fashioned laws still held women back.

In many states, a woman couldn't get a credit card in her own name. Nor could she go to a bank and apply for a loan on her own—she needed her husband's permission. Some state laws said it was a husband's right to choose where the family lived. Women were shut out of countless jobs everywhere. And when they did get jobs, they were often paid less or fired for being pregnant.

Ruth knew firsthand how it felt to be treated unfairly. Now, as a lawyer, she had the power and skills to fight for equal rights in court. First, she started at her own school. Ruth helped female professors at Rutgers file a lawsuit for equal pay. They won.

Next, she signed on as a volunteer lawyer at the American Civil Liberties Union. The ACLU is a group that fights for citizens' basic rights. In addition to full-time teaching, Ruth now started to defend clients and go to court. She did it all for free.

AMERICAN CIVIL LIBERTIES UNION

What Ruth wanted was to "do something" to make a difference in society.

Meanwhile, in the busy Ginsburg home, Ruth and Marty continued living on equal terms. "Growing up, I didn't know that it was unusual for both parents to have careers," James said later.

"People would always ask me what my dad did, and I always wondered why people didn't ask me about my mom."

As to whether Ruth was a devoted mother, James said, grinning, "[Mom] was always there when I wanted her to be—and even when I didn't."

CHAPTER 6
Landmark Cases

One winter afternoon in 1973 found Ruth climbing a set of huge marble steps. Ahead of her towered sixteen white marble columns. Carved above the columns was a famous phrase: "Equal justice under law." This was the Supreme Court

Building in Washington, DC. And Ruth was going inside to argue her first case there!

She wore her mother's circle pin. Thinking of Celia gave her courage. Still, she felt terribly nervous. She hadn't dared to eat lunch for fear of being sick.

A hush fell over the court when it was time to begin. Everyone rose as the nine justices—all men—dressed in long black robes walked in. Could Ruth convince them of her case?

Her client was Sharron Frontiero, an officer in the US Air Force. Male officers received benefits for their wives—such as payments for housing and medical care. However, the air force would not give Frontiero's husband the same benefits. Why? Simply because the lieutenant was female.

Sharron Frontiero

Ruth's voice wobbled a bit when she first addressed the justices. But it grew steady and firm as she launched into her argument. Ruth told the Court that women—not just men—were now breadwinners. A woman's paycheck—and benefits—were just as important as a man's. It was time for the law to catch up to society.

Usually the justices interrupted lawyers with questions. This time, the bench stayed quiet. "The justices were just glued to her," said a lawyer who was present. "I don't think they were expecting . . . [the] sheer force of her argument."

Ruth ended with a quotation. The words were first spoken way back in 1837 by a woman named Sarah Grimké. The quote showed how long American women had fought for equality: "I ask no favor for my sex. All I ask of our brethren is that they take their feet off our necks."

Ruth's argument convinced the court and won the case for Sharron Frontiero! The victory was important for every woman in the United States. From then on, US military forces had to give all women, not just Frontiero, the same benefits as men. And in the future, the government couldn't have one set of rules for men and a different set for women.

Ruth wasn't about to stop now. She searched

for other cases to bring to the Supreme Court. Some involved the rights of men—for example, men who chose to stay home to take care of their children. In the past, lawmakers assumed all caretakers were female. So they made laws that gave stay-at-home mothers, but not fathers, certain rights.

The nine justices on the Supreme Court were all male. Ruth figured that they might identify more easily with a man's experience. And tearing

Supreme Court justices in 1973

down laws that treated men unfairly automatically helped women as well. It made the sexes equal, which was the whole point.

In 1975, Ruth fought for a father named Stephen Wiesenfeld. He wanted to stay home

and take care of his infant son. Stephen's wife had died giving birth, so Stephen was the baby's only parent. The US government said that if a woman lost her husband and stayed home to take care of the family, the government would pay her certain benefits. Yet the government refused to pay Stephen the same benefits.

At the Supreme Court hearing, Ruth sat Stephen right beside her. Again, Ruth argued a powerful case. She showed how laws based on gender hurt everyone—men, women, and children. Several months passed before the Court announced their decision. Ruth heard the verdict on the car radio while driving to school. (By this time, she was teaching law at Columbia University.)

It was a unanimous victory!

Ruth talked about the excitement she felt: "When I got to Columbia, I went running through the halls kissing the students who had worked with me on the case. And I am normally a very unemotional person."

Altogether, during almost ten years, Ruth argued six historic cases before the Supreme Court, winning five! She also wrote the briefs (arguments) for dozens of other important cases. Ruth did something that was "incredibly important to American women—whether they knew it or not," said legal expert Nina Totenberg.

CHAPTER 7
From Lawyer to Judge

President Jimmy Carter, who took office in 1977, noticed something lopsided about the federal courts. There were ninety-seven male judges—and only one woman. The president began a search for well-qualified female candidates to balance the score. One name kept coming up: Ruth Bader Ginsburg. So in 1980, Carter made Ruth a federal judge on a circuit court. Not in

Ruth with President Jimmy Carter, 1980

New York. In Washington, DC. What an honor for Ruth!

Her life changed in major ways. Ruth had to stop teaching. And she could no longer argue cases as a lawyer. Instead, she would sit on the judge's bench in front of lawyers and rule on their cases. Her personal opinions wouldn't matter anymore. To be fair and just, a judge must decide cases based on facts alone.

Ruth and Marty left New York City, their home for so many years, and moved to the nation's capital. Marty took a new job teaching law at Georgetown University. At cocktail parties that the Ginsburgs attended, guests automatically reached to shake Marty's hand when the host introduced "Judge Ginsburg." Marty had to explain that his wife—not he—was the judge. Did Marty feel jealous? Did he mind leaving his old job and following Ruth to DC? Not one bit. "I have been supportive of my wife since the

beginning of time, and she has been supportive of me," Marty said. "It's not sacrifice; it's family." Marty was as confident as ever about his role. In a well-known photo, he posed in his chef's apron beside his wife, who wore a judicial robe.

For the next thirteen years, Ruth proved herself a fair-minded judge. She ruled on cases in a group of three judges. Behind the scenes, Ruth worked hard to get the other judges to agree on verdicts and to speak with one voice.

Another huge turn in Ruth's life came in 1993. An opening had just come up on the Supreme Court. President Bill Clinton was looking for a new justice to fill the slot. Ruth was too shy to brag about her own accomplishments. But Marty wasn't! He did everything possible to make sure President Clinton heard about Ruth's remarkable

work. It landed her an interview with the president. After talking to Ruth about the law for just a few minutes, President Clinton knew he had found the right person for the job.

President Bill Clinton

Federal Courts

A federal law is a law that applies to everybody in the United States. Making counterfeit money, for instance, is a federal crime. When a person or a group breaks a federal law or goes against the Constitution, the case is heard in a *federal court*. (If someone breaks a state law, the case goes to a *state court* instead.)

The United States has three kinds of federal courts. You can think of them set up like a triangle. At the "base" are *district courts*—ninety-four altogether. If a federal law is broken, the case goes to a district court in that state. A jury decides the case. Lawyers who lose can ask for an appeal. That means the case will be heard by the next level of courts—a *circuit court*. (This is the kind of court that Ruth served on.)

Circuit courts are the middle layer of the

triangle. There are only thirteen circuit courts spread out across the nation. Cases are decided by a group of three judges, not by juries.

What if a circuit court disagrees with the verdict of the district court? Lawyers can then ask the *Supreme Court* to settle the disagreement. The Supreme Court sits at the top of the triangle. Its verdict is final.

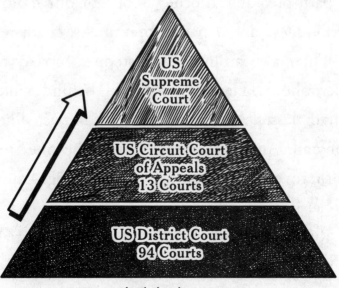

The federal courts

It was nearly midnight that night when Ruth got a call. President Clinton was on the phone! He told Ruth the extraordinary news: She was his choice to become the next justice on the Supreme Court of the United States! This is the greatest honor any American lawyer or judge can receive.

The next day, in front of news cameras at the White House Rose Garden, President Clinton introduced Ruth to the world. He praised her as "a path-breaking attorney," "one of our nation's best judges," and "a person of immense character."

Then a beaming Ruth stepped up to the microphone. Her eyes sparkled behind violet-tinted glasses. A silk scarf tied back her usual neat ponytail. And her mother's pin—the one she'd worn to every Supreme Court hearing—shone on her jacket.

Ruth thanked several people, especially Marty—"my best friend and biggest booster." In closing, she thanked her mother, "the bravest and

strongest person I have ever known. . . . I pray
that I may be all that she would have been had
she lived in an age when women could aspire and
achieve, and daughters are cherished as much as
sons." Moved by her words, the president wiped a
tear from his cheek.

One more hurdle lay ahead before Ruth could take her place on the bench. The Senate still had to confirm her nomination.

Four days of grilling followed. Ruth appeared calm and confident. She answered the senators' questions openly and honestly, even on thorny topics. "I hope my answers please the [Senate]," she said, "but in the end, I am what I am."

Ruth also talked openly about her life. She told the senators she was "a Brooklyn native, born and bred." She related her parents' immigrant past. And she described the hurt of seeing the anti-Jewish sign as a child. Grateful for the United States' freedoms, she said, "What has happened to me could happen only in America."

Ruth won over Democrats and Republicans alike. With resounding approval, the Senate voted in her favor, 96–3!

On August 10, 1993, President Clinton swore in Ruth as a Supreme Court justice. Marty held the Bible for Ruth as she gave her oath to support and defend the Constitution of the United States.

One of the first to welcome Ruth to the bench was Sandra Day O'Connor, the first woman to ever serve on the Supreme Court. O'Connor was overjoyed to have a "sister in law."

Sandra Day O'Connor

CHAPTER 8
"Oyez! Oyez! Oyez!"

Justice Ruth Bader Ginsburg arrived at her first Supreme Court hearing in October 1993.

"Oyez! Oyez! Oyez!" called out the marshal to open the court session. (*Oyez* means "Hear ye!" It's pronounced "oh-yay.") Everyone in the

courtroom stood as the nine justices entered and took their seats. As the newest justice, Ruth sat at the far end of the long, curved bench. She was easy to spot. Ruth, along with Sandra Day O'Connor, wore a white lacy collar over her black robe.

It didn't take long for Ruth to speak up. "The Supreme Court's new term is off to a roaring start," observed one famous lawyer and writer. "In her first hour on the bench, [Ginsburg] asked seventeen questions." This was more than some judges asked in weeks!

Collars Tell a Story

A judge's robe was designed for men to wear. It has an opening at the neck for a shirt and tie. So Ruth wears lace or beaded collars to give the robe  some female flair. (Sandra Day O'Connor started the tradition.) Beyond fashion, Ruth's many collars "speak" a language all their own. A white lace collar tells people she agrees with the winning side. Her black beaded bib collar lets people know she disagrees. A gold collar dangling with beads means she will announce the majority opinion.

Ruth loved her new job. "I think I have the best job in the world for a lawyer," she said. But the workload was fierce! A team of four young clerks and two secretaries helped out. Some of her staff juggled work and caring for young kids at home, just as Ruth used to do. (Now her younger child, James, was twenty-eight.) So Ruth let her staff set their own hours.

Countless decisions had to be made every day, starting with which cases the Supreme Court would hear. The Court receives thousands of appeals. It can only decide on about 150 each year. Ruth, along with the other justices, accepts the cases that have far-reaching effects across the nation.

In 1996, a case came to the Court that had special meaning for Ruth. A famous military school, Virginia Military Institute (VMI), wanted to remain all male. They said female students would "destroy" the school. Ruth disagreed. If a young woman could handle VMI's tough program, she should get the chance, Ruth believed.

The majority of justices agreed with Ruth. Because of her long history in women's rights, she had the honor of reading the Court's opinion from the bench. (An opinion is the Court's verdict.) It was one of her proudest moments.

The nine justices on the Court formed a close-knit "family." Their unique job brought them together for a lifetime, or until one or another retired. Sometimes they disagreed—sharply. Ruth never responded in anger. That just wasted time and energy. She knew differences of opinion were bound to happen on the Court. After all, it was complicated to interpret the US Constitution.

US Constitution

It was written in 1787, when many modern issues were unheard of. Minority rights, the environment, and unions are just a few.

Once Ruth decided on a case, she had to get at least four other judges to agree with her. The majority rules on the Court. Five out of nine justices have to agree in order for a case to win.

Strong opinions didn't stop the justices from getting along. Ruth said the Supreme Court is one of the friendliest places she has ever worked. That's proven in the robing room before every court session.

The robing room is like the justices' "locker room." Their robes are kept there, inside personal lockers. Ten minutes before court time, they gather to slip their robes on over their street clothes. Then a special ritual takes place. It started back in the 1800s. Every justice goes around the room, shaking hands with the other eight. Ruth says it shows "we are in this together and we revere the court and want to leave it in as good shape as we found it."

Antonin Scalia and Ruth Bader Ginsburg

A busy schedule kept Ruth glued to her desk— until Marty came to her chambers (office) and coaxed her home. On weekends, the two enjoyed an active social life in Washington, DC. Opera remained their favorite outing. "When I am at an opera I get totally carried away," said Ruth. Backstage visits with the cast were one of the perks of being a well-known justice. Ruth even got to appear in one opera wearing a white wig. (Of course, she didn't sing.)

Vacations still sometimes brought out Ruth's daredevil side. She parasailed in southern France, white-water rafted down the rushing Colorado River, and water-skied every chance she got. Ruth didn't do anything halfway, whether it was work or play!

CHAPTER 9
"I Dissent!"

By 2013, Ruth had already served on the Supreme Court for twenty years. But it wasn't until that year that her fame exploded.

It started with a court session on June 25, 2013. Ruth wore her black beaded collar to court that day. It meant "Watch out!" Chief Justice John Roberts read aloud an opinion agreed upon by five justices, a majority. It stripped away parts of the Voting Rights Act. Congress had passed the Voting Rights Act nearly fifty years earlier to make sure that minorities got to cast their votes. This was especially important in

Chief Justice John Roberts

states where there had been a long history of preventing certain people from voting. But Chief Justice Roberts said, "Our country has changed." According to the Court's majority opinion, the protections of the past were no longer necessary.

"I dissent!" said Ruth when the chief justice finished. (To *dissent* means to strongly disagree with an opinion.) Her voice was soft as usual, but the dissent she read aloud spoke with a roar.

Discrimination still caused harm in our society, Ruth insisted. (*Discrimination* means acting unfairly to people because of such things as their race or religion or gender.) The Voting Rights Act had done a good job of protecting voters all across the country. Destroying the law now would be "like throwing away your umbrella in a rainstorm because you are not getting wet."

The force of her words rang true to a great many citizens. Suddenly, there was a website calling Ruth "the Notorious RBG." (A rap star had gone by a similar name.) Soon the first RBG T-shirt appeared, followed by a rap song praising Ruth and her work. All these were created by young people who saw Ruth as a hero who spoke truth to power.

Overnight, the justice, who had fought for people's rights for decades, became the rock star of the Court. Her picture and initials popped up everywhere—on greeting cards, mugs, totes, bobblehead dolls, action figures, baby clothes, and even tattoos. A popular saying about Ruth also went viral: "You can't spell truth without Ruth."

Ruth had never sought fame. Now, she good-naturedly accepted being a pop-culture hero. "I'm eighty-four years old and everyone wants to take a picture with me," she said, laughing. The best part was seeing young people use the power of the Internet to make worthwhile social change.

Usually, Ruth agrees with the majority of justices. "We are unanimous much more often than we divide five to four," she points out.

Still, she's not afraid to dissent if she believes the majority is wrong. Her dissents have power. The written record of her words can influence future courts. The voting public listens, too. Citizens can vote for the changes that Ruth urges.

Congress Hears Ruth's Dissent

In 2007, the Supreme Court ruled against a woman named Lilly Ledbetter, a factory manager in Alabama. One day at work, Ledbetter discovered her pay was far less than the pay of male managers. Even men she had trained earned more than she did. So Ledbetter filed a lawsuit. Too late, the Court said in their ruling. She was supposed to file her complaint three months after getting her first paycheck. Instead, she had done it years later.

Ruth dissented. From the bench, she called on Congress to fix the loophole in the federal law. Congress listened, agreed, and took action. The Ledbetter Fair Pay Act became the first bill that President Barack Obama signed into law in 2009. A picture of the signing hangs in Ruth's chambers today.

Is it hard on Ruth when the Court overrules something very important to her? "I'm dejected, but only momentarily," she said. "But then you go on to the next challenge and you give it your all. You know that these important issues are not going to go away. They are going to come back again and again. There'll be another time, another day."

CHAPTER 10
RBG Today

In 2018, Ruth celebrated her twenty-five remarkable years on the Supreme Court. She was eighty-five years old. Is Ruth ready to retire? Not at all. She can still pull all-nighters when work piles up.

What's her secret for keeping in fighting shape? Workouts with her trainer of twenty years, Bryant Johnson. His nickname for the justice is TAN—"tough as nails." Ruth's rigorous routine includes twenty push-ups (knees off the floor), solid planks, and pumping iron. Classical music or the evening news plays in the background.

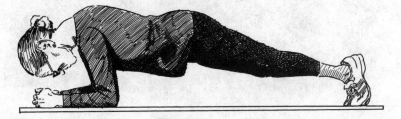

Countless honors and awards have come Ruth's way. One of her favorites was an honorary degree from Harvard Law School—the degree she missed out on when she moved to New York. At the ceremony, the famous opera tenor Plácido Domingo suddenly began to serenade her! The memory was a glorious high point.

In 2018, a popular documentary movie about Ruth's life, *RBG*, was shown at theaters nationwide. It was followed by a film about her pioneering legal work for women's rights, called *On the Basis of Sex.*

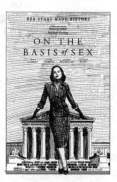

In 2010, Ruth lost her beloved husband, Marty, to cancer. He had been her "best friend" for fifty-six happy years. Her family life remains full and active with her grown kids and four grandchildren. Following in her mother's footsteps,

Jane attended Harvard Law School and went on to teach at Columbia University. James runs a classical music company in Chicago. Ruth's grandkids warmly call their famous grandmother Bubbie (say: BUB-bee).

Sometimes Ruth speaks to students and young workers. She encourages them to "do something outside yourself . . . something to make life a little better for people less fortunate than you. That's what I think a meaningful life is—living not for oneself, but for one's community."

Doesn't that sound just like the life Ruth herself has always led?

Timeline of Ruth Bader Ginsburg's Life

1933 — Joan Ruth Bader is born in Brooklyn, New York

1950 — Celia Amster Bader dies at age forty-seven,
one day before Ruth's high-school graduation

1954 — Marries Marty Ginsburg

1955 — Daughter, Jane Ginsburg, is born

1956 — Enrolls at Harvard Law School

1957 — Marty becomes seriously ill with cancer

1958 — Ruth transfers to Columbia University Law School
in New York City

1959 — Graduates from Columbia at the top of her class

1963 — Rutgers Law School hires Ruth to teach

1965 — Son, James Ginsburg, is born

1972 — Cofounds the Women's Rights Project, a division of the
American Civil Liberties Union

1973 — Argues her first case in front of the US Supreme Court

1980 — President Carter appoints Ruth as a judge on the US Court
of Appeals in Washington, DC

1993 — Nominated by President Bill Clinton for the US Supreme
Court

— Sworn in on August 10

2018 — Celebrates her twenty-fifth anniversary on the
US Supreme Court

Timeline of the World

1789 — The US Constitution institutes the Supreme Court

1837 — A series of letters by Sarah Grimké urging equality of the sexes is published

1868 — The Fourteenth Amendment to the Constitution grants voting rights to men of all races

1920 — The Nineteenth Amendment wins women the right to vote

1941 — In December, the United States enters World War II; the war ends in 1945

1950 — Harvard Law School admits its first women students

1967 — Thurgood Marshall becomes the first African American justice on the Supreme Court

1969 — Apollo 11 lands on the moon

1975 — Bill Gates of Microsoft writes the program for the first personal computer

1981 — Sandra Day O'Connor becomes the first woman justice on the Supreme Court

2009 — In January, Barack Obama becomes the United States' first black president

— In May, he nominates Sonia Sotomayor for the Supreme Court, the first Hispanic person to serve on the Court

2010 — President Obama appoints Elena Kagan to the Supreme Court

Bibliography

*Books for young readers

*Ayer, Eleanor H. ***Ruth Bader Ginsburg: Fire and Steel on the Supreme Court.*** New York: Dillon Press, 1994.

Carmon, Irin, and Shana Knizhnik. ***Notorious RBG: The Life and Times of Ruth Bader Ginsburg.*** New York: HarperCollins, 2015.

De Hart, Jane Sherron. ***Ruth Bader Ginsburg: A Life.*** New York: Alfred A. Knopf, 2018.

Ginsburg, Ruth Bader. ***Ruth Bader Ginsburg: In Her Own Words.*** Helena Hunt, ed. Chicago: Agate Publishing, 2018.

*Henry, Christopher. ***Ruth Bader Ginsburg.*** New York: Franklin Watts, 1994.

Hirshman, Linda R. ***Sisters in Law.*** New York: Harper, 2015.

*Krull, Kathleen. ***No Truth Without Ruth: The Life of Ruth Bader Ginsburg.*** New York: Harper, 2018.

"The Supreme Court; Transcript of President's Announcement and Judge Ginsburg's Remarks." ***New York Times***. June 15, 1993. https://www.nytimes.com/1993/06/15/us/supreme-court-transcript-president-s-announcement-judge-ginsburg-s-remarks.html.

West, Betsy, and Julie Cohen, directors. ***RBG***. New York: Storyville Films and CNN Films, 2018.

*Winter, Jonah. ***Ruth Bader Ginsburg: The Case of R.B.G. vs. Inequality.*** New York: Abrams Books for Young Readers, 2017.